W9-DGO-660

To:_____

From:_____

Date:_____

Other titles in the *Simple Wisdom of…*™ series:

Simple Wisdom of…Love
Simple Wisdom of…Faith
Simple Wisdom of…Living
Simple Wisdom of…Success
Simple Wisdom of…Family
Simple Wisdom of…Aging
Simple Wisdom of…Marriage

SIMPLE WISDOM
OF FRIENDSHI

Created by Marge McDonald and Richard J. Lenz

Illustrations by Addison

Longstreet
Atlanta, Georgia

Published by LONGSTREET PRESS, INC.
A subsidiary of Cox Newspapers
A division of Cox Enterprises, Inc.
2140 Newmarket Parkway, Suite 122
Marietta, Georgia 30067

In addition to being found in fine bookstores, Longstreet books are available for special
sales or promotions. For information please call Special Sales, 800-927-1488, or write:
Special Sales, Longstreet, 2140 Newmarket Parkway, Suite 122, Marietta, GA 30067.

Copyright © 1999 by McDonald & Lenz, Inc.
Design by Lenz Design & Communications, Inc., Decatur, GA

Printed in the United States of America, 1st printing, 1999.

Library of Congress Card Catalog Number: 99-61770

ISBN: 1-56352-573-9

*In many cases we've taken a little liberty with poets' and writers' lines to fit this book
but credited them where we knew who wrote the basic words. We sincerely hope
in their wisdom they forgive us.*

A good thought is indeed a great boon for which God is to be first thanked; next he who is the first to utter it, and then, in a lesser, but still in a considerable degree, the friend who is the first to quote it to us.

—*Bovee*

Animals are such agreeable friends—they ask no questions, they pass no criticisms.

—*George Eliot*

Associate yourself with friends of good quality
if you esteem your own reputation; for 'tis better to be alone
than in bad company.
—*George Washington*

A friend when you're goin' t' seed
is a friend indeed.
—*Abe Martin*

A thousand friends is not enough,
and one enemy is too many.
—*Dr. Frank Crane*

A Father's a treasure;
a Brother's a comfort;
a Friend is both.
—*Benjamin Franklin*

Against a foe I can myself defend,
But Heaven protect me
from a blundering friend.
—*D'Arcy W. Thompson*

A true Friend is the best Possession.
—*Benjamin Franklin*

A friend is a person with whom I may be sincere.
Before him I may think aloud.
—*Ralph Waldo Emerson*

A true friend is the most precious of all possessions
and the one we give least thought in acquiring.
—*Francois, Duc de La Rochefoucauld*

A freeloader is a confirmed guest. He is the man
who is always willing to come to dinner.
—*Damon Runyon*

A friend may well be reckoned the masterpiece of Nature.
—*Ralph Waldo Emerson*

An old friend
is the best mirror.
—*Spanish saying*

Alas! Today I would give everything
To see a friend's face, or hear a voice
That had the slightest tone
of comfort in it.
—*Henry Wadsworth Longfellow*

As steel sharpens steel,
so a friend sharpens a friend.
—*Proverbs*

A friend means well,
even when he hurts you.
But when an enemy puts his arm
around your shoulder—watch out!
—*Proverbs*

Actions, not words, are the true criterion
of the attachment of friends.
—*George Washington*

A true friend is forever a friend.
—*George Macdonald*

Always choose for your friend
one that is wise and good,
and just, Ingenious and honest,
and in those things
which have a latitude.
—*Jeremy Taylor*

A constant in all other things is friendship,
Save in the office and affairs of love.
—*William Shakespeare*

As old wood is best to burn,
an old horse to ride,
old books to read,
and old wine to drink,
so are old friends
always the most trusty.
—*Leonard Wright*

A friend is one who knows
all about you
and loves you all the same.
—*Elbert Hubbard*

Be not forgetful to entertain strangers, for you may entertain angels unawares.
—*Hebrews*

Be agreeable! And you'll be in demand.
For in every walk of life
friendships are crying out
for the agreeable person.
—*Dr. Frank Crane*

Be slow in cussing a friend,
slower in changing one.
—*Benjamin Franklin*

Best friend, my well-spring
in the wilderness!
—*George Eliot*

Brothers may not be Friends,
but a Friend will always be a Brother.
—*Benjamin Franklin*

Books are life-long friends
whom we come to love and know
as we do our children.
—*S. L. Boardman*

Be not the first by whom the new are try'd
Nor yet the last to lay the old friend aside.
—*Alexander Pope*

Beware of those that traffic
in incense and in poisons;
that is, of flatterers and backbiters.
—*Oriental saying*

Best to remember:
Elephants never forget.
Daisies don't tell.
Two things we humans
might well take to heart.
—*Robert Benchley*

Books *are* friends, and what friends they are!
Their love is deep and unchanging;
their patience inexhaustible;
their gentleness perennial;
and their sympathy
without selfishness.
—*John Langford*

A **Companion's** words of wisdom can be persuasive.
—*Ovid*

DEVIL'S PLUNGE →

Defend me from my friends; I can defend myself from my enemies.
—*Marschal Villars*

Everyone

can have a friend,
Who himself knows
how to be a friend.
—*Tiedge*

Friends are like melons. Shall I tell you why? To find a good one, you must a hundred try.

—*Claude Mermet*

FRESH
FRIENDS

Friendship can truly be said to be
what makes all other things work!
—*Dr. Frank Crane*

Friendship is Love without wings.
—*Lord Byron*

From my foe, as from my friend, comes good;
My friend shows what I can do, and my foe what I should.
—*Johann von Schiller*

Friendship cannot live with Ceremony, nor without Civility.
—*Benjamin Franklin*

Friendship, like love, is but a name,
Unless to one you stint the flame.
—*John Gay*

Familiarity is at the root of the most affectionate friendships
and the strongest hatreds.
—*Antonine Rivaroli*

Friendship is a compact by which we undertake
to do someone small favors
in expectation of receiving big favors.
—*Charles de Secondat*

For I am the only one of my friends
that I can rely upon.
—*Appolodorus*

Friends are worthless who know how to receive a favor,
but not how to return one.
—*Plautus*

Friendship eases and unloads the mind,
clears and improves the understanding,
engenders thoughts and knowledge,
animates virtue and good resolutions, soothes and allays the passions,
and finds employment for most of the vacant hours of life.
—*Joseph Addison*

Friendship is a sheltering tree.
—*Coleridge*

Friendship, one soul in two bodies.
—*Pythagoras*

Forgive friends when they wrong you.
Remembering those wrongs will break up a friendship.
—*Proverbs*

Friendship is listening when needed
but it doesn't mean you need all the answers.
—*Anonymous*

"Friend" is sometimes a word devoid
of meaning, "enemy," never.
—*Victor Hugo*

Friend of my bosom, you more than a brother,
Why wer't you born in my father's house?
—*Charles Lamb*

Friendship! Mysterious cement of the soul! Sweet'ner of life!
—*Robert Blair*

Favors are pleasant so long
as they are of a kind we can return
or they can destroy friendship.
—*Caius Cornelius Tacitus*

Friendship born of love
is better
than love itself.
—*French saying*

Friends who promise things
that they never give
are like clouds and wind
that bring no rain.
—*Proverbs*

Friendship
of two men
is the deepest
and highest sentiment
of which the
finite mind is capable.
—*Gertrude Franklin Atherton*

God gave us relatives; thank God we can choose our friends.
—*Addison Mizner*

Go often to a house of a friend for weeds will choke the unused path.
—*Ralph Waldo Emerson*

Good friends, good books and a sleepy conscience: this is the ideal life!
—*Mark Twain*

Genuineness and Modesty are the Keys of Friendship.
—*Dr. Frank Crane*

Good friends are worth more than good relatives.
—*Spanish saying*

Good friends know how to compliment us
just "to the saturation-point."
—*Dr. Frank Crane*

Good nature is more agreeable
in conversation than wit,
and gives a certain air to the countenance
which is more amiable than beauty.
—Joseph Addison

Greater love hath no man than this,
that a man lay down his life for his friends.
—*Book of John*

God can bestow nothing more sacred upon us than friendship!
It enhances every joy, mitigates every pain.
Everyone can have a friend,
Who himself knows how to be a friend.
—*Christopher Agustus Tiedge*

Goodness: nothing is so popular.
—*Benjamin Franklin*

Give your ear to all,
your hand to your friends,
but your lips
only to your wife.
—*Yiddish saying*

Good books are the best of friends,
the same today and forever.
—*Martin Farquhar Tupper*

31

Having a friend is having another self.
—*Socrates*

He deserves paradise who makes his companions laugh.
—*The Koran*

Have many acquaintances,
but few friends.
—*Spanish saying*

Humor crosses all boundries with friends.
—*Irish saying*

Hold faithfulness and sincerity as first principles.
Have no friends not equal to yourself.
—*Confucius*

He gain'd from Heav'n, a friend.
'Twas all he wish'd.
—*Thomas Gray*

He who bestows his goods upon the poor or friends,
Shall have as much again, and ten times more.
—*John Bunyan*

How good it feels!
The hand of an old friend.
—*Henry Wadsworth Longfellow*

Hearts that are delicate and kind and tongues
that are neither—
these make the finest company.
—*Logan Pearsall Smith*

He who has a thousand friends
has not a friend to spare,
And he who has one enemy
shall meet him everywhere.
—*Ali Ben Abu Taleb*

He who believes everybody will be bitten,
but he who believes nobody will be devoured.
—*Reverend Charles Spurgeon*

He that lends to his friends
loses double.
—*Italian saying*

If I can ease one life from aching, or cool one pain, Or help one fainting robin into his nest again, I shall not live in vain.

—*Emily Dickinson*

I was angry with my friend;
I told my wrath,
my wrath did end.
—*William Blake*

It is better to be loyal than to be affectionate.
—*Dr. Frank Crane*

I do not wish to treat friendships daintily,
but with roughest courage.
When they are real, they are not glass threads
or frost-work, but the solidest
thing we know.
—*Ralph Waldo Emerson*

In friendship every burden's light.
—*John Gay*

It is one of the most beautiful compensations
of this life that no man can sincerely try
to help another without helping himself.
—*Ralph Waldo Emerson*

In the life of the young the most essential thing for happiness
is the gift of friendship.
—*William Osler*

I would not enter on my list of friends
(though graced with polish'd manners and fine sense,
yet wanting in sensibility) the man who needlessly
sets foot upon a worm.
I have loved my friends,
as I do virtue,
My soul, my God.
—*Sir Thomas Browne*

In all thy humours, whether grave or mellow,
thou'rt such a touchy, testy, pleasant fellow.
Thou hast so much wit and mirth and spleen about thee
that there's no living with thee or without thee.
—*Joseph Addison*

I do with my friends as I do with my books.
I would have them where I can find them,
but I seldom use them.
—*Ralph Waldo Emerson*

A difference of taste in Jokes
is a great strain upon
the affections of friends.
—*George Eliot*

Keep company with the wise and you will become wise. If you make friends with stupid people, you will become stupid.
—*Proverbs*

Friend: one who knows all about you and **loves** you just the same.

—*Elbert Hubburd*

Love is only chatter,
Friends are all that matter.
—*Gelett Burgess*

Life without a friend is death without a witness.
—*Spanish saying*

Love, friendship, philosopher's stone,
These three things men value alone.
—*Henrich Heine*

Laughter is not at all a bad beginning for a friendship,
and it is far the best ending for one.
—*Oscar Wilde*

Life is to be fortified by many friendships.
—*Anonymous*

To love and to be loved,
is the greatest happiness of existence.
—*Sydney Smith*

Let your friendships be immortal
and your hates mortal.
—*Livy*

Literary friendship is a sympathy
not of manners,
but of feelings.
—*Isaac Disraeli*

Let there be truth between us two forevermore…
It is sublime to feel and say of another,
I need never meet, or speak, or write to him;
we need not reinforce ourselves,
or send tokens of remembrance;
I rely on him as on myself;
if he did thus or thus, I know it was right.
—*Ralph Waldo Emerson*

Lend money to an enemy,
and thou'lt gain him;
To a friend,
and thou'lt lose him.
—*Benjamin Franklin*

Make up your mind
to let your friends have their
peculiarities…and they will
let you have yours!
—*Anonymous*

My friend, more divine than all divinities.
—*George Eliot*

Most friendships of the world
are often Confederacies in vice,
or leagues of pleasure;
Ours has the severest virtue for its basis,
And such a friendship ends not but with life.
—*Joseph Addison*

My friends have come to me unsought.
The great God gave them to me.
—*Ralph Waldo Emerson*

Mary's mouth costs her nothing,
For she never opens it
at others' expense.
—*Benjamin Franklin*

More years had made me
love thee more.
—*Alfred Tennyson*

Making friends, who are real friends,
is the best token of a man's success in life.
—*Edward Everett Hale*

Men who are quarrelsome
have no good neighbors.
—*Benjamin Franklin*

Magnets in our hearts will attract true friends.
That magnet is unselfishness,
thinking of others first...
When you learn to live for others, they will live for you.
—*Paramahansa Yogananda*

Monkeys, warm with envious spite,
their most obliging friends will bite.
—*Benjamin Franklin*

Men fear silence as they fear solitude,
because both give them a glimpse
of the terror of life's nothingness.
—*Andre Maurois*

True friendship is never without anxiety.
—*Marie de Rabutin-chantal*

Old friends are best.
King James called for his old
shoes because they were
easiest on his feet.
—*John Selden*

Our friends know us in prosperity, in adversity we know our friends.
—*Anonymous*

O friends, whom chance and change can never harm.
—*Barry Cornwall*

Of all plagues, good Heaven, your wrath can send,
Save, save, oh!
Save me from the candid friend.
—*George Canning*

On the choice of friends
Our good or evil name depends.
—*John Gay*

Our friendship is like the beautiful shadows of evening,
Spreading and growing.
—*Michael Vitkovics*

One friend is worth a hundred relatives.
—*Dr. Frank Crane*

Of all the heavenly gifts that mortals commend,
What trusty treasure in the world can countervail a friend?
—*Nicholas Grimoald*

Our friends are worth all hazards we can run.
—*Charles Young*

One's mind never unbends itself so agreeably
as in the conversation of a well-chosen friend.
—*Joseph Addison*

O friend! O best of friends! Thy absence more than the impending night
darkens the landscape o'er!
—*Henry Wadsworth Longfellow*

Old friendships are the wine of life.
—*Charles Young*

Our pleasures have a higher relish
when they are rarely used.
—*Juvenal*

Pleasant words between friends are valued and do not cost much.
—*Italian saying*

There are plenty of **acQuaintances** in the world, but very few real friends.

—*Chinese moral maxim*

Remember,

it is not so much our friends' help that helps us as the confident knowledge that they will help us.

—*Epicurus*

Reward of virture is virtue; the only way to have a friend is to be one.
—Ralph Waldo Emerson

Real friendships begin with liking or gratitude—roots that can be pulled up.
—George Eliot

Real friendship is realized when silence between friends is golden.
—Italian saying

Real friends never have to declare their love.
—Henry David Thoreau

Reconciled friendship is a double enemy.
—Spanish saying

Refuse to lend, and make an enemy; lend, and make an eternal enemy.
—Russian saying

Real friends never give your name t' an agent of any kind.
—Abe Martin

Rotten apples
spoil their companions.
—*Benjamin Franklin*

Real friendship eases and unloads the mind,
clears and improves the understanding,
engenders thoughts and knowledge,
animates virtue and good resolutions,
soothes and allays the passions,
and finds employment for most of the vacant hours of life.
—Joseph Addison

Regret is an appalling
waste of energy;
you can't build on it;
it's good only for wallowing in.
—*Katharine Mansfield*

Remember that the entire population
of the universe,
with one trifling exception,
is composed of others.
—*John Andrew Holmes*

Silence is
the virtue of
friends who are
not wise; so, when
you know speak
out.
—*French saying*

So long as we are loved by others,
I would almost say that we are indispensable;
no one is useless while they have a friend.
—*Robert Louis Stevenson*

Some friendships are made by nature,
some by contact,
Some by interest,
and some by souls.
—*Jeremy Taylor*

Sincerity is the sacrament of friendship.
—*Arabian saying*

Save a friendship...forgive and forget!
—*Irish saying*

Sweeter none than a voice of a faithful friend;
Sweet always, sweetest heard in the loudest storm.
Some I remember,
and will ne'er forget.
—*Edward Pollok*

Seldom do we know the true value of friends.
While they live, we are too sensitive
of their faults;
When we have lost them,
we only see their virtues.
—*J. C. and A. W. Hare*

Sell upon trust and you will lose
many friends
and always
want money.
—*Benjamin Franklin*

So, if I live or die to serve my friend,
'Tis for my love,—'tis for my friend alone,
And not for any rate that friendship bears
In heaven or on earth.
—*George Eliot*

Some worth it argues,
a friend's worth to know;
Virtue to own the virtue of a foe.
—*Benjamin Franklin*

There is indeed no blessing of life that is any way comparable to the enjoyment of a discreet and virtuous friend.

—*Joseph Addison*

The holy passion of Friendship is of so sweet and steady, loyal,
and enduring a nature that it will last through a whole lifetime,
if not asked to lend money.
—*Mark Twain*

The secret to making friends that will last long
is to be a long time
making them.
—*Greek saying*

The making of friends, real friends,
is the best measure of a person's success in life!
—*Edward Everett Hale*

The moment of finding a fellow creature
is often as full of mingled doubt and exultation,
as the moment of finding an idea.
—*George Eliot*

The same man cannot be
both Friend and Flatterer.
—*Benjamin Franklin*

Three faithful friends—an old wife,
an old dog, and ready money.
—*Benjamin Franklin*

The only safe way to destroy an enemy is to make him your friend.
—*Mark Twain*

Those friends thou hast,
Grapple them to thy soul
With hoops of steel.
—*Shakespeare*

The greatest friendships are self made.
A friend means well, even when he hurts you.
But when an enemy puts his arm
around your shoulder—watch out!
—*Proverbs*

The poor make few new friends;
But O, they love the better still
Those few our Father sends.
—*Lady Dufferin*

The greatest of all sufferings is jealousy,
and the one that arouses the least pity
is the friend who causes it.
—*Francois, Duc de La Rochefoucauld*

There are three friendships which are advantageous:
Friendship with the upright;
friendship with the sincere;
and friendship with those of observation.
—*Confucius*

To cast away a virtuous friend,
I call as bad as to cast away one's own life,
which one loves best.
—*Theodore Buckley*

Trust not too much in a new friend
or in an old house.
—*German saying*

The only way to have a friend is to be one.
—*Ralph Waldo Emerson*

True happiness consists not
in the multitude of friends,
But in the worth and choice.
Nor would I have virtue a popular regard pursue:
Let them be good that love me,
though but few.
—*Ben Jonson*

True friendship's laws are by this rule express'd,
Welcome the coming, speed the parting guest.
—*Alexander Pope*

To act the part of a true friend requires more conscientious feeling than to
fill with credit and complacency any other station or capacity in social life.
—*Mrs. Sarah Ellis*

There is no treasure which may be compared to a faithful friend.
—*Anonymous*

True love may be rare,
but it is far less rare than true friendship.
—*Francois, Duc de La Rochefoucauld*

True friendship is a plant of slow growth,
and must undergo and withstand
the shocks of adversity,
before it is entitled
to the appellation.
—*George Washington*

The essence of friendship is entireness,
a total magnanimity and trust.
—*Ralph Waldo Emerson*

Time, which makes most things ugly,
makes friendship beautiful.
—*French saying*

There is nothing that is meritorious
but virtue and friendship.
—*Alexander Pope*

Treasures are not friends,
but a friend is a treasure.
—*French saying*

Take the advice of a faithful friend,
and submit thy inventions
to his censure.
—*Thomas Fuller*

True happiness is of a retired nature,
and an enemy to pomp and noise;
it arises, in the first place,
from the enjoyment of ones self;
and, in the next,
from the friendship and conversation
of a few select companions.
—*Joseph Addison*

Time, which strengthens friendship,
weakens love.
—*Jean de La Bruyére*

'Tis better to leave an enemy
at one's death,
than beg of a friend
in one's life.
—*Benjamin Franklin*

'Tis great confidence
in a friend to tell him
your faults,
greater to tell him his.
—*Benjamin Franklin*

The mind never unbends itself
so agreeably
as in the conversation
of a well-chosen friend.
—*Joseph Addison*

The wise man draws
more advantage from his enemies,
than the fool
from his friends.
—*Benjamin Franklin*

There are plenty
of acquaintances
in the world,
but very few real friends.
—*Chinese moral maxim*

The man who hails you Tom or Jack,
And proves by thumping
on your back
His sense of your great merit,
Is such a friend,
that one had need
Be very much his friend indeed
To pardon
or to bear it.
—*William Cowper*

'Tis sweet, as year by year
we lose Friends out of sight,
in faith to muse
How grows in Paradise
our store.
—*Reverend John Keble*

The friendship between me and you
I will not compare to a chain;
for that the rains might rust,
or the falling tree
might break.
—*George Bancroft*

Using money to help a friend is a good reason for having it.
—*Anonymous*

Visitors

and Fish stink after three days.

—*Benjamin Franklin*

What

are friends for if not to share love in times of trouble.

—*Proverbs*

Who is great? He who turns an enemy into a friend.
—*The Talmud*

Whatever the number of a man's friends,
there will be times in his life when he has one too few;
But if he has only one enemy, he is lucky indeed if he has not one too many.
—*Edward Bulwer-Lytton*

Wisely spoken words can heal the wounds
made deep by thoughtless words.
—*Anonymous*

We that live to please, must please to live.
—*Samuel Johnson*

Whoever knows how to return a kindness he has received, must be a
friend above all price.
—*Theodore Buckley*

Women give to friendship only what they borrow from love.
—*Sebastien-Roch-Nicholas Chamfort*

When arguing with a friend, stop and think what is right,
not who is right.
—*Proverbs*

Welcome a new neighbor with your favorite recipe
and invite them to your home for a cup of coffee and chat.
—*Anonymous*

We can live without a brother, but not without a friend.
—*German saying*

Who ceases to be a friend, never was one.
—*Aristotle*

While you are secure and happy you will have many friends;
When your life has adversity, only true friends will remain.
—*Homer*

We secure our friends not by accepting favors
but by doing them.
—*Thucydides*

If you are eXceptionally poor at most things, save being a true friend, then you are rich at something of exceptional importance.
—*Mark Kershaw*

**You** mistake my fortunes; I am wealthy in my friends.
—*Timon of Athens*

You never have to say I'm sorry for that which
you were wise enough not to say.
—*Benjamin Franklin*

Yes, a friend who suffers alone offends his friend.
—*Antoine Gombaud*

You should eat and drink with a friend,
but do no business with him.
—*Turkish saying*

Yes, we must ever be friends; and of all who offer you friendship let me
be ever the first, the truest, the nearest and dearest!
—*Henry Wadsworth Longfellow*

Your friendship is infinitely better than kindness.
—*Cicero*

You must love me, myself, and not my circumstances,
if we are to be real friends.
—*Charles Yonge*

You cannot be friends upon any other terms
than upon the terms of equality.
—*Woodrow Wilson*

You will be careful, if you are wise,
how you touch men's religion, credit, or eyes.
—*Benjamin Franklin*

You will forgive me, I hope, for the sake of the friendship between us,
Which is too true and too sacred to be so easily broken!
—*Henry Wadsworth Longfellow*

You can'st not joke an enemy into a friend but thou may'st
a friend into an enemy.
—*Benjamin Franklin*

You shall judge of a man by his foes as well as by his friends.
—*Joseph Conrad*

You may regret your silence once, but you will regret your talk twice.
—*Yiddish saying*

Zeal of fools or friends offends at any time…
—*Alexander Pope*

WELCOME BACK CLASS OF '80

He that is an agreeable friend lights up the room like a lamp. He is like love when you are lonesome, bed when you are tired, a breeze when you are stifling, and money when you are broke.

—*Dr. Frank Crane*